AFRO-BETS™

1 2 3

BOOK

by

Cheryl Willis Hudson

AFRO-BETS™ is a trademark of Cheryl Willis Hudson. The AFRO-BETS™ Kids were conceived and created by Wade Hudson and Cheryl Willis Hudson. Pictures are rendered by Culverson Blair after original illustrations by the author. Inquiries should be addressed to JUST US BOOKS, a division of Just Us Productions, Inc., 301 Main Street, Orange, NJ 07050.
Printed in the United States of America   First Edition   Library of Congress Catalog Card Number 87-82952   ISBN: 0-940975-01-7

one yellow sun

1

one

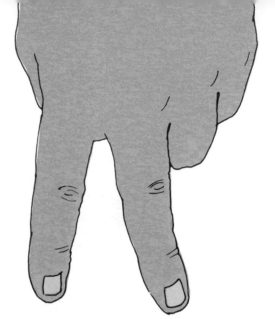

two blue shoes

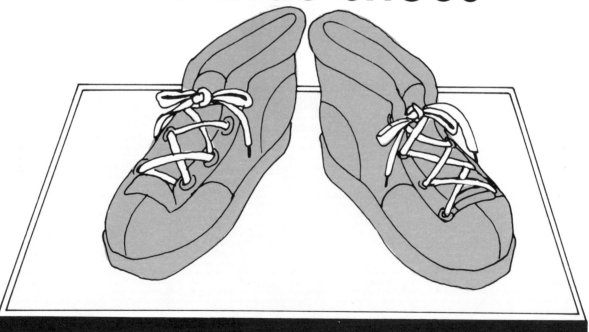

2

two

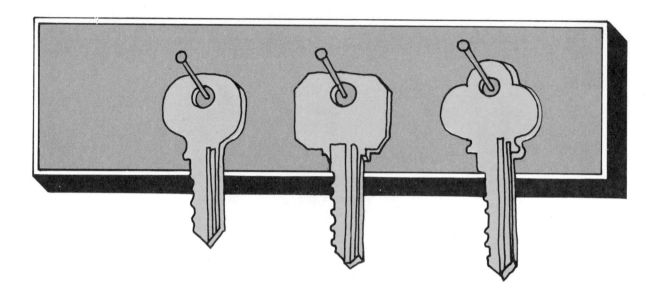

three gold keys

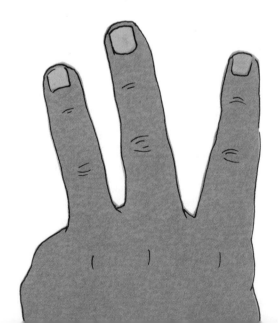

3

three

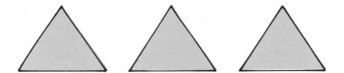

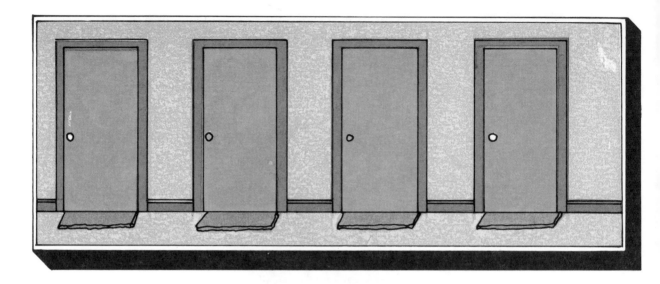

four green doors

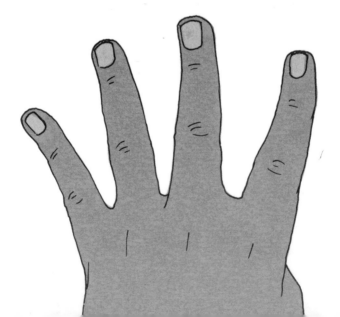

4

four

five apple pies

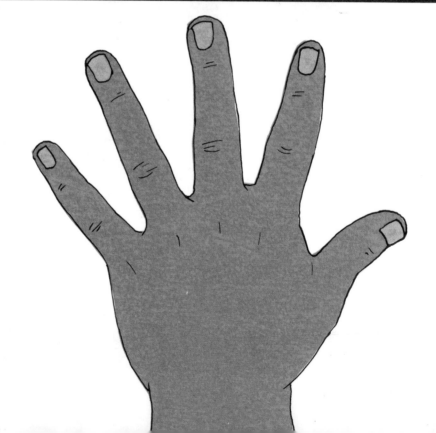

5   **five**

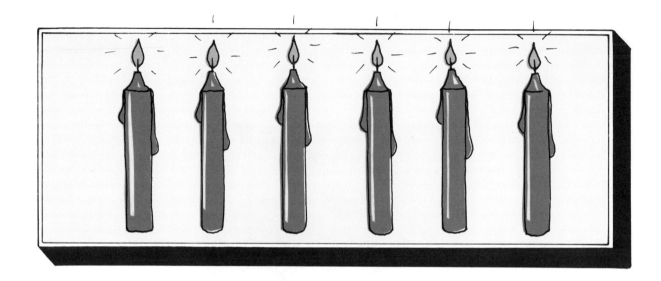

six candlesticks

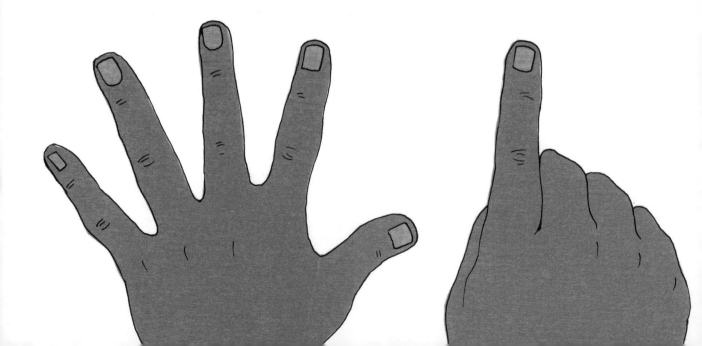

6

six

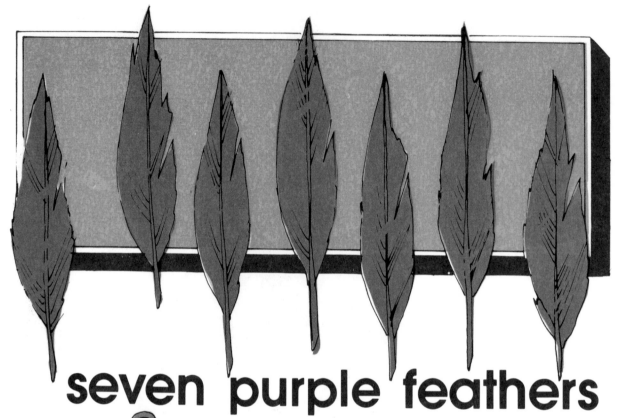

seven purple feathers

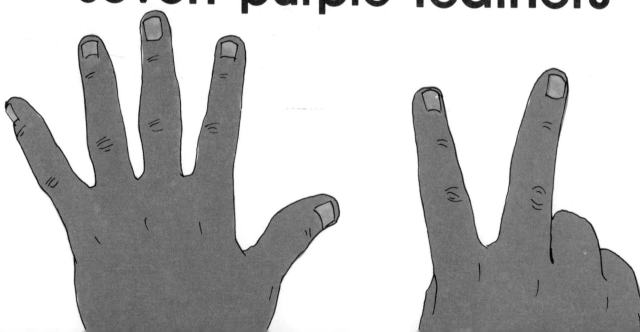

7 seven

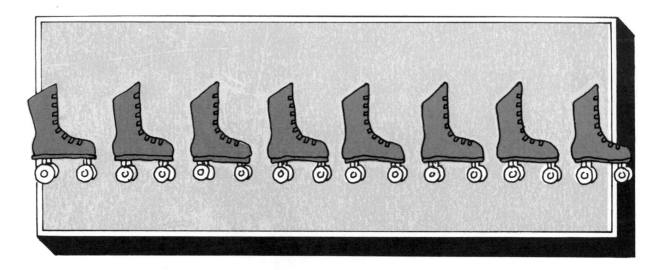

eight roller skates

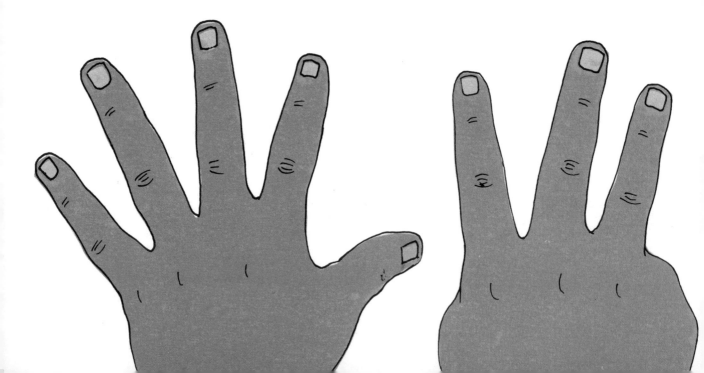

8

eight

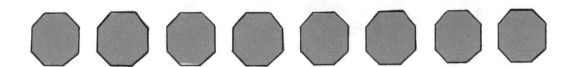

nine silver dimes

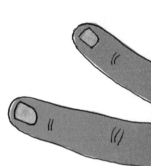

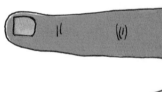

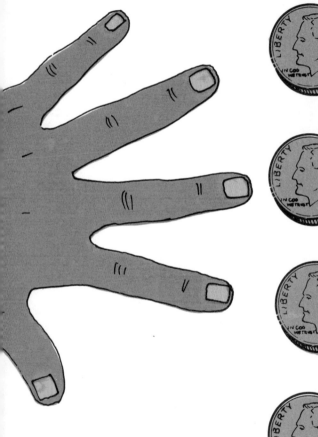

9 nine

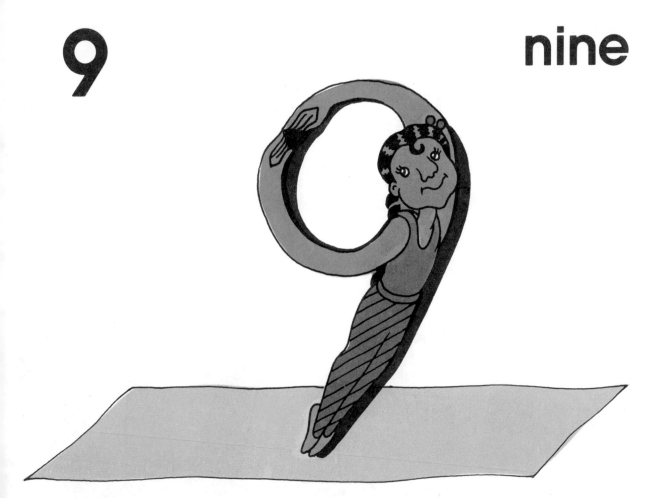

ten red hens

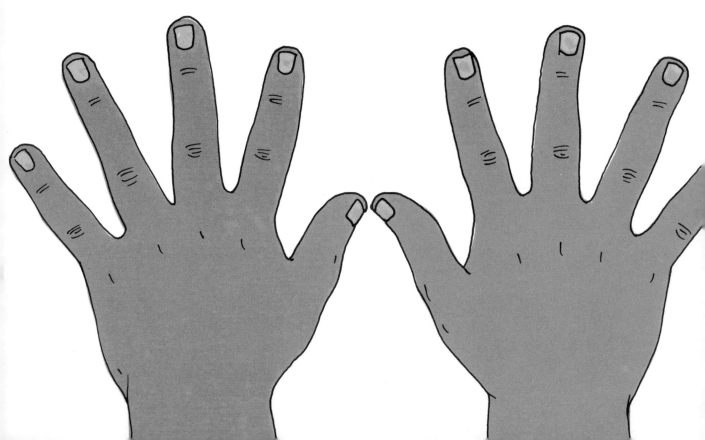

10

ten

How many?

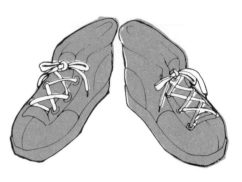

____ shoes

____ sun

____ keys

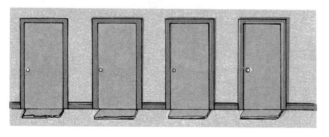

____ doors

____ pies

1 2 3 4 5

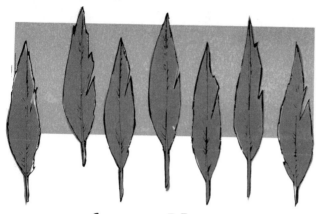

___ **feathers**

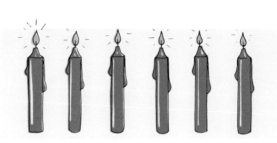

___ **candle-sticks**

___ **skates**

___ **dimes**

___ **hens**

6   **7**   **8**   **9**   **10**

Review your numbers
with the **AFRO-BETS**™ Kids.

 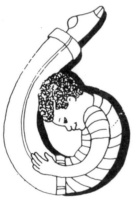